HAMLET

It is a cold, dark night outside the King of Denmark's castle, and the guards are trying to keep warm. Suddenly they see a ghost! They have seen it twice before. It is the ghost of the dead King, Hamlet's father, who died very suddenly a short time ago. The guards are worried, and a little afraid. Perhaps the ghost wants to say something important, so they decide to tell Hamlet about it.

Inside the castle, Hamlet's uncle Claudius, who is now the King, is drinking and laughing with his new wife Gertrude, Hamlet's mother. They both want Hamlet to be happy, like them, but he can't forget his father, and is still wearing black. 'I want to die!' he thinks. 'How empty life is!'

But when he sees the ghost, and hears what it has to tell him, he is no longer sad, but angry. Now the only thing that matters to him is revenge! There will be a death in the castle very soon.

D1296188

OXFORD BOOKWORMS LIBRARY

Playscripts

Hamlet

Stage 2 (700 headwords)

Playscripts Series Editor: Clare West

WILLIAM SHAKESPEARE

Hamlet

Retold by
Alistair McCallum

OXFORD UNIVERSITY PRESS

OXFORD
UNIVERSITY PRESS

Great Clarendon Street, Oxford OX2 6DP

Oxford University Press is a department of the University of Oxford.
It furthers the University's objective of excellence in research, scholarship,
and education by publishing worldwide in

Oxford New York

Auckland Cape Town Dar es Salaam Hong Kong Karachi
Kuala Lumpur Madrid Melbourne Mexico City Nairobi
New Delhi Shanghai Taipei Toronto

With offices in

Argentina Austria Brazil Chile Czech Republic France Greece
Guatemala Hungary Italy Japan Poland Portugal Singapore
South Korea Switzerland Thailand Turkey Ukraine Vietnam

OXFORD and OXFORD ENGLISH are registered trade marks of
Oxford University Press in the UK and in certain other countries

This simplified edition © Oxford University Press 2008

Database right Oxford University Press (maker)

First published in Oxford Bookworms 2004

2 4 6 8 10 9 7 5 3

No unauthorized photocopying

ISBN 978 0 19 423517 4

A complete recording of this Bookworms edition of
Hamlet is available on audio CD ISBN 978 0 19 423523 5

Printed in Hong Kong

Photos supplied by Ronald Grant Archive and reproduced
courtesy of Carlton International Media Limited/LFI

For more information on the Oxford Bookworms Library,
visit www.oup.com/bookworms

CONTENTS

INTRODUCTION

Hamlet is set in Denmark, a country in the north of Europe. Before the play begins, Hamlet's father, the King, died suddenly and his brother Claudius became the new King. Claudius married his brother's wife, Queen Gertrude.

PERFORMANCE NOTES

Act 1   Scene 1: Outside the castle
            Scene 2: A room in the castle
            Scene 3: Laertes' room
            Scene 4: Outside the castle

Act 2   Scene 1: Polonius's room
            Scene 2: A room in the castle

Act 3   Scenes 1 and 2: A room in the castle
            Scene 3: Claudius's room
            Scene 4: Gertrude's room

Act 4   Scene 1: Gertrude's room
            Scene 2: A room in the castle

Act 5   Scene 1: Outside the castle
            Scene 2: A room in the castle

You will need some swords, some bags for Laertes, chairs and tables, a few letters and books, a small box, a crown, a small bottle, some flowers, a spade, a skull, some wine-bottles, some cups, and some black clothes for Hamlet. You will need something like a hole in the ground for a grave, and something that looks like blood. In Gertrude's room there must be a large curtain for Polonius to hide behind.

CHARACTERS IN THE PLAY

Hamlet, Prince of Denmark

Claudius, King of Denmark, brother of Hamlet's dead father

Gertrude, Queen of Denmark, Hamlet's mother and Claudius's wife

The ghost of Hamlet's dead father

Polonius, adviser to Claudius

Laertes, Polonius's son

Ophelia, Polonius's daughter

Horatio, a friend of Hamlet's

Rosencrantz and **Guildenstern,** friends of Hamlet's when he was younger

Bernardo, Francisco and **Marcellus,** guards at the King's castle

A grave-digger

Other guards and servants

Three actors

Hamlet

The dead King comes back

It is dark. Francisco, a guard, is standing outside the King's castle. He is looking around and listening.

FRANCISCO How cold and dark it is! I'm tired, and I want to go to bed. *(He hears a noise.)* What was that noise? Who's there?

BERNARDO *(Entering)* Don't worry, Francisco – it's me, Bernardo. Is everything all right?

FRANCISCO Yes. It's been very quiet. What time is it?

BERNARDO It's midnight. You can go to bed now. You look tired. Horatio and Marcellus will be here soon.

FRANCISCO I think that they're coming now. I can't see anyone, but I can hear voices. *(Horatio and Marcellus enter.)* Stop! Who's there? Is that you, Horatio?

HORATIO Yes, Francisco, it's me.

MARCELLUS And me. We've come to see Bernardo.

FRANCISCO He's here with me. Well, I'm going. Goodnight, everyone. *(He leaves.)*

BERNARDO Horatio! Marcellus! It's good to see you both.

1

HORATIO Bernardo, you know why we've come. Marcellus says that you've seen a ghost out here.

MARCELLUS We've seen it twice, haven't we, Bernardo?

HORATIO I don't believe you! Ghosts aren't real. You only find them in stories.

BERNARDO The ghost is real, Horatio. Marcellus and I saw it last night, at about one o'clock.

The ghost enters.

MARCELLUS Look! It's come again! Look over there!

HORATIO It's the King! It's the dead King! I can't believe my eyes!

BERNARDO Speak to it, Horatio. You're cleverer than us. We don't know what to say.

HORATIO *(To the ghost)* Who are you? What are you? What do you want? Speak to us!

MARCELLUS It's moving away.

HORATIO Stop! Tell us why you have come! Is there something that we must do? Is there going to be trouble in Denmark? *(The ghost leaves.)* Don't go!

BERNARDO Shall we follow it?

MARCELLUS No. It's gone. It won't come back tonight.

BERNARDO It'll be morning soon. They say that ghosts never walk during the day.

HORATIO Shall we tell Prince Hamlet about this? It was the ghost of his dead father, the King. It didn't speak to us, but it will speak to him, I'm sure.

MARCELLUS Yes, let's find Hamlet and tell him.

ACT 1 SCENE 2
Hamlet is thinking about his father

Inside the castle. King Claudius is talking. Gertrude is next to him, with their servants. Hamlet, Polonius and Laertes are listening. Hamlet is wearing black clothes.

CLAUDIUS The death of my dear brother has made us all very sad, and everyone in Denmark will remember him for a long time.

POLONIUS That is very true, my lord.

CLAUDIUS But life must go on, and, as you all know, I have married my brother's wife, Gertrude. Hamlet, you are like a son to me now.

'Hamlet, you are like a son to me now.'

GERTRUDE Hamlet, your clothes are black, like the night. Why do you still look so unhappy?

HAMLET Do I *look* unhappy, mother? Perhaps I *am* unhappy. I can change my clothes, but I can't change what I feel.

GERTRUDE Try not to think about your father any more, Hamlet. Let your eye look on Claudius as a friend. Remember – all that lives must die.

CLAUDIUS Don't be sad, Hamlet. Your father lost a father, and that father lost his. Death is everywhere. Think of me as your father now. Come with me, everyone. We will drink to my new family!

They all leave, but Hamlet stays.

HAMLET Oh, God! I want to die! How empty life is! My father, the greatest man in Denmark, has gone. The man who's taken his place is no better than an animal. Oh, mother! Why did you marry him? Break, my heart!

Horatio, Marcellus and Bernardo enter.

HORATIO My lord, we have some important news for you.

HAMLET Horatio! Good to see you! You've been away, haven't you?

HORATIO Yes, my lord. But I came back to Denmark for your father's funeral.

HAMLET Or was it my mother's wedding? *(He laughs*

angrily.) Horatio, in my mind's eye I can still see my father.

HORATIO My lord . . . I saw him last night.

HAMLET What! That's not possible!

HORATIO We saw a ghost last night, my lord.

HAMLET Where was it? And what was it like?

MARCELLUS It was outside the castle, my lord.

BERNARDO It looked like the dead King, my lord.

HORATIO I knew your father, my lord. It was him.

HAMLET What did it do? What did it say?

'What did it say?'

MARCELLUS It came near to us and looked at us, but it didn't speak.

HAMLET If it is the ghost of my father, perhaps it will speak to me. I must see this ghost.

BERNARDO Marcellus and I have seen it three times, my lord, at midnight or later.

HORATIO Perhaps it will walk again tonight, my lord.

HAMLET I'll meet you all tonight at midnight, outside the castle. Don't tell anyone what you have seen!

ACT 1 SCENE 3
Ophelia makes a promise

Laertes is in his room with his sister Ophelia. He is packing his bags for a journey.

LAERTES Well, Ophelia, I'm ready to go. You'll write to me while I'm studying in France, won't you?

OPHELIA Of course I will, Laertes.

LAERTES Before I go, I must talk to you about Hamlet. Tell me the truth: has he told you that he loves you?

OPHELIA He is very friendly to me. He has given me presents, and . . .

LAERTES Don't believe him, Ophelia! He uses beautiful words, and perhaps he likes you now, but he doesn't really love you.

'Hamlet doesn't really love you.'

OPHELIA Doesn't he? But . . .

Polonius enters.

POLONIUS Hurry, Laertes! Your ship is ready to leave!

LAERTES I'm ready, father.

POLONIUS Before you go, I want to tell you a few things, because you haven't been away from home before. You must be careful. Don't make friends too quickly; take your time. Don't get into fights too easily.

LAERTES I'll be careful, my lord.

POLONIUS Give every man your ear, but few your voice.

LAERTES I'll remember what you say, father. Now, I'm ready to leave, so . . .

POLONIUS Neither a borrower nor a lender be; you will lose either your money or your friend. Above all, be true to yourself; it must follow, as night follows day, that you cannot be untrue to other people. Now, hurry!

LAERTES Goodbye, father. Goodbye, Ophelia – and remember what I told you! *(He leaves.)*

POLONIUS What did he mean, Ophelia?

OPHELIA We were talking about Hamlet before you came in, my lord.

POLONIUS Ah! I have been worried about this. You spend too much time alone with him, my dear.

OPHELIA But he is very kind to me, my lord.

POLONIUS Kind? Surely you don't think that he loves you?

OPHELIA I do not know what to think, my lord.

POLONIUS Ophelia, Hamlet is a prince. One day he will marry someone important. His fine words mean nothing. I want you to stay away from him. Don't talk to him any more! Do you understand?

OPHELIA Yes, father. I won't see him again, I promise.

ACT 1 SCENE 4
The ghost speaks

Hamlet, Horatio, Marcellus and Bernardo are outside the castle. It is dark.

HAMLET How cold it is! Is it midnight yet, Horatio?

HORATIO Yes, my lord. Perhaps we'll see the ghost soon. *(There is a noise inside the castle.)* What was that?

HAMLET Claudius is drinking with his friends, as usual. They're all shouting and dancing. Sometimes he drinks all night, Horatio.

The ghost enters.

HORATIO Look, my lord! Look, here it comes again!

HAMLET *(To the ghost)* Are you good or bad? I don't know, but I will speak to you. King, father, answer me! Why have you come back from the grave? *(The ghost moves away and looks back at Hamlet.)* He wants me to follow.

HORATIO My lord, don't follow him!

MARCELLUS It's dark and dangerous out here, my lord!

BERNARDO You'll have an accident, my lord!

HAMLET I'm going to follow him. I'm not afraid. It doesn't matter if I die. *(The others try to stop him.)* Leave me alone! *(He pulls out his sword.)* I'll make a ghost of anyone who tries to stop me!

Hamlet follows the ghost. The others try to follow, but they go the wrong way. Hamlet is alone with the ghost.

HAMLET Speak to me, and I will listen.

GHOST Hamlet, I am the ghost of your dead father. There is something that you must do. If you loved your father . . .

HAMLET Oh, I did, I did!

GHOST You must take revenge for his terrible murder.

HAMLET Murder! Oh, tell me who murdered my father, and I will kill him!

GHOST Everyone thinks that a snake killed me. But it's not true. The snake that killed me now wears my crown.

HAMLET What! So the murderer was Claudius!

GHOST Yes – my brother! While I was sleeping in the garden, he put poison in my ear. He took my life, my crown, and my wife. Don't hurt your mother, Hamlet. But you must take revenge on Claudius!

HAMLET I will, I will!

GHOST Remember! *(The ghost leaves.)*

HAMLET Remember? How can I ever forget? Claudius will die – I won't rest until that day!

Horatio, Bernardo and Marcellus enter.

BERNARDO Here he is!

MARCELLUS We tried to follow you, my lord.

HORATIO What news, my lord? Did the ghost speak to you?

HAMLET Yes, Horatio, he told me a secret, a terrible secret. One day I'll tell you what he said, but not yet. *(He takes out his sword.)* Now, put your hands on my sword. Promise that you won't tell anyone about the ghost.

They hear the ghost's voice.

GHOST Promise!

HORATIO, MARCELLUS and BERNARDO We promise.

MARCELLUS I can hear the ghost, but I can't see it.

BERNARDO Where is it? Is it under the ground?

HORATIO This is strange, my lord.

HAMLET You are a clever man, Horatio, but there is more in this world than you can ever dream of.

HORATIO That's true, my lord.

HAMLET Listen, all of you. For a while, the things that I say and do will be strange and unusual. Perhaps people will even think that I am mad. Promise that you will not say anything about me.

GHOST Promise!

HORATIO, MARCELLUS and BERNARDO We promise.

HAMLET Now, let's go back into the castle.

Act 2 Scene 1
A strange visit

Polonius is alone in his room.

POLONIUS Well, Laertes has left. I hope that he . . .
Ophelia runs into the room.
POLONIUS Ophelia! What's the matter, my dear?
OPHELIA I've just had a terrible surprise. Hamlet . . .
POLONIUS Now, my dear, I told you not to talk to the Prince, didn't I?
OPHELIA Yes, father, but he came into my room. He didn't knock – he just walked in.
POLONIUS And what did he say? What did he do?
OPHELIA He didn't say anything. He just looked at me.
POLONIUS He didn't hurt you, did he?
OPHELIA No, father. He just stood in front of me and held my arm. He was shaking. Perhaps he's ill?
POLONIUS No, my dear, it's worse than that, I think. Come with me. We must talk to the King.

Act 2 Scene 2
Hamlet meets two old friends

In the castle. Claudius and Gertrude are talking to Rosencrantz and Guildenstern.

CLAUDIUS Rosencrantz and Guildenstern, thank you for coming to see us. The Queen and I would like your help.

GERTRUDE You were at school with Hamlet, weren't you?

ROSENCRANTZ Yes, my lady, we've known him for a long time.

GUILDENSTERN How can we help, my lord?

CLAUDIUS Hamlet is very unhappy. Of course, he was sad – like all of us – when his father died. But I don't think that is the only problem.

GERTRUDE We want you to stay with the Prince for a while. Talk to him. Try to find out why he is so worried. Will you help us?

GUILDENSTERN Of course, my lady. We will do all that we can.

GERTRUDE Thank you. But we need help quickly. Can you talk to my son soon?

ROSENCRANTZ We will find Hamlet at once, my lady.

Rosencrantz and Guildenstern leave. Polonius enters.

CLAUDIUS Ah, here's Polonius. Have you any news?

POLONIUS Yes, my lord, I have some news about Hamlet.

CLAUDIUS Good! We want to help him, Polonius.

POLONIUS Well, my lord, I believe that I know what has happened to him. As you know, I have a daughter, Ophelia. *(He takes out a letter.)* She gave me this.

GERTRUDE Is it from Hamlet?

POLONIUS Yes, my lady. Listen. *(He reads.)* 'To the beautiful Ophelia . . . never forget that I love you. I cannot count how many times I have cried . . .'

CLAUDIUS It's a love letter! So Hamlet loves your daughter?

POLONIUS Yes, my lord. He has loved her for some time.

GERTRUDE What about Ophelia? Does she love him?

POLONIUS I don't know, my lady, but I told her not to talk to the Prince, not to answer his letters, and not to keep his presents.

CLAUDIUS Do you think that his love for Ophelia has made him unhappy?

POLONIUS Yes, my lord, but it's worse than that. He is not just unhappy – he is ill, perhaps even mad.

GERTRUDE Mad? My poor son! What can we do?

Hamlet enters, reading a book.

POLONIUS He's coming now! We'll decide what to do later.

Claudius and Gertrude leave.

POLONIUS What are you reading, my lord?

HAMLET Words, words, words.

POLONIUS Can I do anything for you, my lord?

HAMLET Yes. You can leave me alone.

Polonius leaves. Rosencrantz and Guildenstern enter.

HAMLET My good friends, Rosencrantz and Guildenstern! I haven't seen you for years! It's good to see you both. What are you doing in this prison?

ROSENCRANTZ Prison, my lord?

'Words, words, words.'

HAMLET Denmark's a prison.

GUILDENSTERN Surely not, my lord?

HAMLET To you it isn't; to me it is. Things are only good
or bad if we think they are. But why have you
come to the castle?

ROSENCRANTZ We've come to see you, my lord.

HAMLET Perhaps someone asked you to come?

GUILDENSTERN What do you mean, my lord?

HAMLET Perhaps the King and Queen want you to ask me
a few questions?

ROSENCRANTZ Well, they have talked to us . . .

GUILDENSTERN It's true, my lord, they asked us to help.

HAMLET Don't worry, I'm not angry. I know that they are
worried. I've been unhappy for some time.

ROSENCRANTZ But why, my lord?

HAMLET I don't know, my friends. Look at the world! How beautiful it is, the sun, the sky, the stars! But to me, it is empty and dead. What a piece of work is a man! How strong and clever, the greatest of God's animals! But to me, man is uninteresting – and so is woman.

ROSENCRANTZ We are sorry that you are so sad, my lord.

GUILDENSTERN Don't forget that there is a play this evening, my lord. Will we see you there?

HAMLET A play? Good! Of course I'll be there. Now, my friends, I want to be alone. I'll see you later.

Rosencrantz and Guildenstern leave.

HAMLET I have an idea. Everyone will be at the play this evening. I'm going to talk to the actors and ask them to change the play a little. The play's the thing that will show the truth about Claudius the King!

ACT 3 SCENE 1
A strange conversation

Claudius, Gertrude, Polonius and Ophelia are in a room in the castle.

CLAUDIUS Gertrude, my love, Polonius and I have a plan.

POLONIUS As you know, my lady, Hamlet is in love with my daughter. His love has made him mad, I think.

CLAUDIUS We're going to listen, secretly, while Hamlet and Ophelia talk. We want to understand what's wrong with the Prince.

GERTRUDE I hope you can help my son. Ophelia, my dear, if you love him, perhaps he will get better.

OPHELIA I hope so, my lady.

Gertrude leaves.

POLONIUS Hamlet will be here soon. *(He gives Ophelia a book.)* Here, my dear, read this book. Then Hamlet won't know that you are waiting for him.

Polonius and Claudius hide. Hamlet enters.

HAMLET To be or not to be, that is the question: to go on living, fighting against this sea of troubles, or to die and end everything? Why be afraid of death? To die is to sleep, no more. Perhaps to dream? Yes, that's the problem: in that sleep of death, what dreams will come? *(He sees Ophelia.)* Oh, beautiful Ophelia!

OPHELIA My lord, are you well? You gave me some presents – I want to give them back.

HAMLET I never gave you anything.

OPHELIA You know that's not true, my lord. You sent letters, too, with beautiful words that made the presents even sweeter. But now you have changed.

'Perhaps I loved you once.'

HAMLET Perhaps I loved you once.

OPHELIA You did, my lord, you did.

HAMLET But perhaps not. No, I never loved you.

OPHELIA Please don't say that! *(She starts crying.)*

HAMLET Love is nothing, Ophelia. You mustn't marry. If you have children, they'll be stupid, like your father.

OPHELIA What are you saying, my lord? What's the matter?

HAMLET *(Shouting)* You women, with your beautiful faces and soft voices! Aren't there any good women left? Ophelia, you must never marry, do you understand? All your life! Not me, not anyone! *(He leaves.)*

18

OPHELIA *(Crying)* What's happened to him? He was a good, kind man, and he loved me. Why has he changed so much?

Claudius and Polonius come out from their hiding-place.

CLAUDIUS Is he in love? Is he mad? I'm not sure, Polonius. But something is wrong.

OPHELIA Father, Hamlet said some terrible things . . .

POLONIUS You don't need to tell us, my dear – we heard everything. Don't cry, Ophelia.

CLAUDIUS I'm worried, Polonius. Hamlet is the Prince – he is an important man. If he goes on saying these strange things, it will be dangerous for all of us.

POLONIUS That's true, my lord.

'I'm worried, Polonius.'

CLAUDIUS If he leaves Denmark for a while, perhaps he will get better. Visiting a different country will be good for him. I'm going to send him away, Polonius. I'm going to send him to England.

POLONIUS Very well, my lord.

ACT 3 SCENE 2
A murder

A room in the castle. Horatio and Hamlet are talking.

HAMLET I've told you what the ghost said, haven't I?

HORATIO Yes, my lord. Do you believe what he said – that Claudius murdered your father?

HAMLET He told the truth, I'm sure. Listen, Horatio. The play's going to start soon. Watch it carefully – and watch Claudius, too.

HORATIO Why, my lord? What's going to happen?

HAMLET I have told the actors to change the play. Remember what the ghost told me – Claudius put poison in my father's ear while he was sleeping.

HORATIO And that's going to happen in the play?

HAMLET That's right! I want to see what happens when Claudius sees the murder. Then we'll know the truth about my father's death, Horatio!

HORATIO I'll watch carefully, my lord.

'Don't worry, mother. It's only a play.'

Claudius, Gertrude, their servants, Polonius, Ophelia, Rosencrantz and Guildenstern enter, and sit down.

CLAUDIUS What play are we going to see, Hamlet?

HAMLET It's a murder, my lord.

GERTRUDE A murder!

HAMLET Don't worry, mother. It's only a play. But it's a
      true story. Here come the actors.

Two actors, playing a king and queen, enter. The king is wearing a crown.

OPHELIA Is it a long play, my lord?

HAMLET No, it's short. As short as a woman's love.

The king and queen kiss. The queen leaves, and the king lies down and sleeps. Another man enters, carrying a small bottle.

21

GERTRUDE   What's he going to do, Hamlet?

HAMLET   We'll have to wait and see, mother.

The man holds the bottle to the king's ear. The king sits up for a second, then falls back, dead. The man puts on the crown.

CLAUDIUS   I don't like this play.

The queen comes back and sees the dead king. She cries. Then the murderer comes to her and kisses her.

CLAUDIUS   *(Shouting)* Stop! No more! *(He runs out.)*

POLONIUS   Stop the play! Now!

Hamlet and Horatio stay, while the others leave.

HAMLET   Did you see how he jumped, Horatio?

HORATIO   Yes, my lord. Now we know the truth!

Horatio leaves.

HAMLET   I haven't forgotten the words of my dead father. I will have my revenge. I want blood – the blood of Claudius!

ACT 3 SCENE 3
Claudius tries to talk to God

Claudius is in his room, talking to Rosencrantz and Guildenstern.

CLAUDIUS   I'm sending Hamlet to England. Rosencrantz and Guildenstern, I want you to go with him.

ROSENCRANTZ Very well, my lord.

CLAUDIUS You must understand that he is a dangerous man. I want you to watch him carefully.

GUILDENSTERN We will, my lord.

CLAUDIUS Go and get ready to leave.

Rosencrantz and Guildenstern leave. Polonius enters.

POLONIUS My lord, I've told Hamlet that his mother wants to talk to him. I'm going to hide in her room while they talk.

CLAUDIUS Good. Perhaps you'll find out what's the matter with him.

Polonius leaves. Claudius is alone.

CLAUDIUS Why did Hamlet want me to see that play? Does he know what I have done? But how can he know? Oh God, I have done a terrible thing. I wanted the crown, and I killed my brother to get it. Oh God, I'm sorry!

Hamlet enters. Claudius has his eyes closed, and does not see him.

HAMLET Shall I kill him now? Yes. Now I can do it. Now I will do it. *(He takes out his sword.)* No, not now. I don't want him to die while he is talking to God. I want his death to be terrible!

He puts his sword back and leaves.

Act 3 Scene 4
A terrible mistake

Gertrude is sitting in her room, talking to Polonius.

POLONIUS I've asked Hamlet to come and see you, my lady. I'll hide behind the curtain while you talk. I want to hear what he says.

GERTRUDE I can hear him coming. Hide now. Quickly!

Polonius hides behind the curtain. Hamlet enters.

HAMLET You want to talk to me, I think.

GERTRUDE Yes, Hamlet. What was that strange play about? Your father is angry and worried.

HAMLET What do you mean, mother? My father is dead.

GERTRUDE Claudius is your father now.

HAMLET I know Claudius better than you think. I know you, too: you are the Queen, your husband's brother's wife. And, I'm sorry to say, you are my mother.

GERTRUDE I'm not going to listen to this!

She tries to stand up.

HAMLET *(Shouting)* Listen! I'm going to tell you the truth!

He pushes her back on her chair.

GERTRUDE Help! Guards!

POLONIUS *(Shouting, from behind the curtain)* Help! Guards! The Queen is in danger!

HAMLET There's someone behind the curtain! *(He takes out his sword and stabs it through the curtain.)*

GERTRUDE Oh, Hamlet! You've killed him!

HAMLET Is it the King? *(He pulls back the curtain. Polonius is dead.)* Polonius!

GERTRUDE Oh, what a bloody thing you have done!

HAMLET Bloody? Yes, nearly as bad, good mother, as killing a king – and marrying his brother!

GERTRUDE Killing a king? What are you talking about?

HAMLET The man you married, mother, is a murderer.

GERTRUDE No! Hamlet! What are you saying?

HAMLET *(Shouting)* Why did you do it? Your husband was a good man, a loving father, a great king – and you married the animal who murdered him!

'Polonius!'

The ghost enters.

GERTRUDE *(Crying)* No more, Hamlet, no more.

HAMLET The ghost of my father! You've come again!

GERTRUDE *(To herself)* My poor son! He's mad!

GHOST Hamlet, don't hurt your mother. I don't want her to be unhappy. But Claudius is still alive. Take revenge, Hamlet! Remember!

GERTRUDE What are you looking at, Hamlet?

HAMLET Can't you see it? My father! Your husband! The King! Look at him! Aren't you afraid?

GERTRUDE There's nothing there, Hamlet.

The ghost leaves.

HAMLET It's gone. I'm not mad, mother. I'm telling the truth. Your husband is a murderer! I'll leave you now. Don't tell anyone what I have said.

GERTRUDE But what shall we do about Polonius?

HAMLET Ha! He always loved talking. But he won't tell any secrets any more!

Hamlet leaves, pulling Polonius's body after him.

ACT 4 SCENE 1
Claudius decides what to do about Hamlet

The Queen is still in her room. Claudius enters.

CLAUDIUS What did Hamlet say, my love? How is he?

GERTRUDE He's mad and angry, like a stormy sea. There was a noise behind the curtain, and he pulled out his sword . . . and killed Polonius!

CLAUDIUS Oh no! He is a danger to us all. Where is he?

GERTRUDE I think that he's gone to hide the body.

CLAUDIUS We must find him. *(Shouting)* Rosencrantz! Guildenstern! *(They enter.)* Find Hamlet! Quickly! He's killed Polonius! *(They leave.)*

GERTRUDE He's sorry for what he has done, I'm sure.

CLAUDIUS This is terrible news, Gertrude. There will be trouble, I'm afraid. I'm sending him away to England. But we will have to explain this death to everyone.

Rosencrantz and Guildenstern enter, with Hamlet and guards.

GERTRUDE Where's Polonius, Hamlet?

HAMLET He's having a rest. A long rest.

CLAUDIUS He's mad, Gertrude. He won't tell us anything.

HAMLET But if you go up those stairs *(showing them)* you'll smell something strange.

CLAUDIUS Guards! Quickly! Go up those stairs and find the body. *(The guards leave.)*

HAMLET There's no hurry – he'll wait.

CLAUDIUS Now, Hamlet, you're going to England soon. Your friends are going with you. You'll feel better if you leave Denmark for a while.

HAMLET England? Good. I'll get ready. *(He leaves.)*

CLAUDIUS Rosencrantz, Guildenstern: I want you to stay with Hamlet all the time. Do you understand?

GUILDENSTERN Yes, my lord. We won't leave him alone.

CLAUDIUS *(Giving Rosencrantz a letter)* When you arrive, you must give this letter to the King of England immediately. It's very important.

ROSENCRANTZ We are your servants, my lord, and will do as you say. *(Rosencrantz and Guildenstern leave.)*

CLAUDIUS *(To himself)* That letter is important. The King of England is my friend. I've asked him to do something for me – kill Hamlet! I will never be happy while that man is alive!

ACT 4 SCENE 2
Some terrible news for Laertes

A room in the castle. Gertrude is talking to a servant.

SERVANT Ophelia isn't well, my lady.

GERTRUDE What's the matter with her?

SERVANT When we told her that her father was dead, she was very sad. Now she's saying strange things.

Ophelia enters.

OPHELIA *(Singing)* Oh, my love is dead, my love is dead, and lying in the ground . . .

GERTRUDE   Ophelia! What's wrong, my dear?

Claudius enters.

OPHELIA   Don't talk. You must listen to my song. *(Singing, dancing)* His clothes were as white as snow, when to his grave he did go . . .

CLAUDIUS   Oh, no! The poor girl is mad! Her father's death was too much for her.

OPHELIA   It's a sad song, isn't it? There are no flowers on his grave. Good night, ladies; sweet ladies, good night. *(She leaves.)*

CLAUDIUS   Follow her! She mustn't be alone. *(The servant leaves.)* Oh, Gertrude! Will our problems never end? *(There is noise and shouting outside.)*

GERTRUDE   What's all that noise? Who's there?

Laertes runs in and pulls out his sword.

LAERTES   *(Shouting)* My father! Who killed my father?

CLAUDIUS   Good Laertes, it's true that your father is dead, and we are all very sad.

LAERTES   Who did it? I'll kill him!

GERTRUDE   Laertes, you must believe me. It wasn't Claudius who killed your father.

LAERTES   Who was it? I'll have my revenge!

CLAUDIUS   Don't worry, Laertes. The man who killed your father will die. Soon!

Ophelia enters, carrying flowers and singing.

LAERTES   Ophelia! Don't you know me?

'Remember. Remember.'

OPHELIA *(Singing)* All the people cry, as in your grave you lie . . . Why aren't you singing?

LAERTES My dear sister! Oh, flower of spring! Is it possible? *(Crying)* She has gone mad!

OPHELIA *(Giving flowers to everyone)* This flower is for you. And this one is for you, and you, and you. Remember. Remember. *(She leaves.)*

CLAUDIUS Gertrude, my dear, leave us for a while. *(Gertrude leaves.)* Laertes, it was Prince Hamlet who killed your father.

LAERTES Hamlet! Where is he?

CLAUDIUS He has gone to England. Don't worry, Laertes, we will hear some news about him soon.

LAERTES When he comes back, I'll kill him!

A servant enters.

SERVANT A letter has arrived, my lord, from Hamlet.

The servant gives Claudius the letter, and leaves.

CLAUDIUS From Hamlet? But . . . that's not possible! *(He reads the letter.)* Oh, no! He's back in Denmark. He's coming here – soon!

LAERTES That's good news!

CLAUDIUS No. Something has gone wrong. I'll have to think of a different plan. Hamlet must die. But it must look like an accident. I have an idea. A sword fight!

LAERTES Yes, my lord, I'm good at fighting.

CLAUDIUS It will be a friendly fight. I'll ask everyone to come and watch. But one of the swords will have poison on it!

LAERTES Everyone will enjoy watching it. They will think that it's just to see who is the better fighter!

CLAUDIUS That's right. But Hamlet will die!

Gertrude enters, crying.

GERTRUDE Oh, Laertes! Your sister! Poor, mad Ophelia!

CLAUDIUS What's happened?

GERTRUDE There's a beautiful, tall tree by the river – the poor girl climbed into it, still singing her sad songs.

LAERTES Oh, no! And did she fall into the water?

GERTRUDE Yes. She's dead, Laertes!

Act 5 Scene 1
Fighting at the funeral

Outside the castle, a man is digging a grave.

GRAVE-DIGGER   Nearly finished. I'm thirsty! *(He drinks, and starts singing.)* Oh, when I was young and in love, the time went too fast . . .

He throws a skull out of the grave, and goes on singing. Hamlet and Horatio enter.

HAMLET   We'll be at the castle soon, Horatio. Wait. What's this? *(Taking the skull)* A skull!

HORATIO   There's a grave-digger over there, my lord.

HAMLET   And he's singing! How funny!

GRAVE-DIGGER   *(Singing)* But now I'm old and grey, and . . .

HAMLET   Whose grave is that?

GRAVE-DIGGER   It's mine. I made it.

HORATIO   No, who is it for?

GRAVE-DIGGER   Oh, it's for a lady. An important lady.

HAMLET   *(Holding the skull)* And whose skull is this?

GRAVE-DIGGER   That was Yorick. He died twenty years ago. Well, I've finished. *(He leaves.)*

HAMLET   Poor Yorick! I knew him well, Horatio. He played with me when I was a child. He was always laughing. No more laughing now, eh, Yorick?

'Poor Yorick!'

HORATIO Someone's coming – let's hide, my lord.

Hamlet and Horatio hide. Claudius, Gertrude, Laertes, servants and guards enter. They are carrying a body.

HAMLET It's the King and Queen! And Laertes! It's a funeral, Horatio. Who has died? Whose body is that?

The servants put the body in the grave.

LAERTES Oh, my dear sister, you died too young.

HAMLET What! Ophelia? Oh, no! Is she dead?

GERTRUDE *(Putting flowers on the body)* Poor girl, I hoped that you would marry my son Hamlet one day.

LAERTES Ah! Don't say that name! Ophelia died because of him! Oh, my beautiful sister, I must kiss you one last time. *(He jumps into the grave.)*

HAMLET *(Shouting)* That's not true! *(He goes up to the grave.)* What are you saying? I didn't kill Ophelia! I loved her!

HORATIO Stop, my lord! *(He runs after Hamlet.)*

LAERTES Hamlet! I'll kill you! You never loved my sister! She was unhappy because of you!

HAMLET I loved her more than you did! Much more!

Hamlet jumps into the grave, and the two men fight.

CLAUDIUS Stop fighting! Guards! Stop them!

GERTRUDE Don't hurt him, Laertes!

The guards pull them out of the grave.

CLAUDIUS Horatio, go back to the castle with Hamlet. Stay with him. *(Hamlet and Horatio leave.)*

GERTRUDE Don't be angry, Laertes. The Prince doesn't know what he is saying. He will be better soon.

CLAUDIUS *(Secretly, to Laertes)* Don't worry. You will have your revenge!

Act 5 Scene 2
Revenge

A room in the castle. Hamlet and Horatio are talking.

HORATIO So you escaped from the ship, my lord?

HAMLET Yes. I found a letter, Horatio, from Claudius to his friend the King of England. Rosencrantz and

Guildenstern were carrying it secretly, but I decided to read it.

HORATIO What did the letter say?

HAMLET You won't believe this, Horatio: it told the King of England to kill me! Immediately!

HORATIO So Claudius killed your father, and now he wants to kill you, because you know the truth!

HAMLET That's right, Horatio. He is a dangerous man. But I will kill him first. And I will tell the world that he murdered the true King!

A servant enters.

SERVANT My lord, Laertes would like to have a sword fight with you. Just a friendly fight – it will be interesting for everyone to watch, he thinks.

HAMLET A sword fight? Yes! Tell him I'll play. *(The servant leaves.)* That's good, Horatio. I like Laertes. I'm sorry that I fought him earlier.

Claudius, Gertrude, Laertes, servants and guards enter.

CLAUDIUS Now, Hamlet and Laertes: shake hands.

GERTRUDE We want you to be friends.

HAMLET Laertes, I was wrong to say those things at the funeral. Please think of me as a friend and a brother.

LAERTES Very well. *(They shake hands.)* Let's start!

CLAUDIUS Bring the swords!

A servant brings two swords.

GERTRUDE   And bring in the wine! If Hamlet wins, I will drink!

The servants bring in some wine and cups.

CLAUDIUS   *(Secretly, to Laertes)* Laertes, take this sword. There's poison on it!

LAERTES   But what if I can't touch him with the sword?

CLAUDIUS   Don't worry. I have put poison in his wine. Hamlet will die!

HAMLET   Come on, Laertes – let's start!

They fight, and Hamlet touches Laertes with his sword.

LAERTES   You win the first time, Hamlet.

CLAUDIUS   Wait a minute. Give this drink to Hamlet! *(He gives a cup to the servant.)* Drink, Hamlet!

HAMLET   Not yet. Are you ready, Laertes?

They fight. Hamlet touches Laertes again.

GERTRUDE   Well done, Hamlet! Are you getting too hot, my dear? Do you want some wine? I'll have some!

CLAUDIUS   Stop! Gertrude! Don't drink!

GERTRUDE   What's the matter, my love?

She drinks from Hamlet's cup.

LAERTES   Come on, Hamlet, let's fight again. *(To Claudius)* Shall I do it now, my lord?

CLAUDIUS   Wait . . . I don't know. The Queen . . .

HAMLET   Come on, Laertes. You aren't trying!

They fight. Laertes stabs Hamlet with his sword.

HORATIO   My lord! There's blood on your face!

HAMLET What's happening? Is he trying to kill me?
Hamlet takes the sword from Laertes and stabs him
angrily. Gertrude falls to the floor. Everyone shouts.

CLAUDIUS Don't worry, she's all right. She feels ill when
she sees blood.

GERTRUDE No! It was the wine! Oh, my dear Hamlet!
She dies.

HAMLET Guards! There's a murderer in here! Lock the
doors!

LAERTES It's too late, Hamlet. You are going to die. No
doctor can help you now. You haven't half an
hour's life left. There was poison on the sword –
and in the drink! It was the King . . . (*He dies.*)

HAMLET   Well, poison, do your work! *(He stabs Claudius.)*

CLAUDIUS   Guards! Guards! Help me!

HAMLET   Murderer! Drink this, and follow my mother into death! *(He puts the cup to Claudius's mouth, and Claudius dies.)* Horatio, I am dying.

HORATIO   And I will die with you, my lord. There is still some poison in the cup. *(He takes the cup.)*

HAMLET   No! *(He pulls the cup away from Horatio.)* Horatio, you must live. I want you to tell the world the truth about me, and Claudius, and my father. Death is coming fast, Horatio – no more words . . . *(He dies.)*

HORATIO   Now breaks a great heart. Good night, sweet Prince. Rest now – the world will know the truth.

GLOSSARY

actor a person who acts in a play, usually in a theatre

adviser someone who gives help and ideas

believe to feel sure that something is true or right

castle a strong building made of stone, often the home of a king or queen

crown something a king or queen wears on his or her head

curtain a large piece of cloth, usually covering a window

dig to make a hole in the ground

dream something that happens in your mind while you are asleep

enter to come in

funeral when family and friends put a dead person's body in the ground

ghost the spirit of a dead person that comes back to visit people

grave a place in the ground where a dead body is buried

guard a soldier who keeps a place (or person) safe

heart a person's feelings and hopes

king the head of a country, or husband of a queen

kiss to touch someone with the lips in a loving way

lady a title for a woman of good family

lend to let someone have or use something for a time

lord a title for a man of good family

mad ill in the mind, unable to think or behave normally

mind the part of you that thinks and understands

play a story (like *Hamlet*) that people can watch, often performed by actors in a theatre

poison something that will kill you or make you very ill

prince the son of a king or queen

problem something that is difficult to understand or deal with

promise to tell someone that you will certainly do something

queen the head of a country, or wife of a king

revenge when you hurt someone who has hurt you

sad unhappy

servant someone who works (for example, cooking or cleaning) in another person's house

skull the bones of your head

snake an animal with no legs, often with a poisonous bite, that moves along the ground

stab to hurt someone with a knife or sword

sword a very long, sharp kind of knife used for fighting

truth something that is true

wedding when a man and woman marry (often in a church)

wine a strong drink made of grapes

Hamlet

ACTIVITIES

Before Reading

1 **Read the back cover of the book. How much do you know now about Hamlet? Circle Y (yes) or N (no) for each sentence.**

1 Hamlet is the King of Denmark. Y / N
2 Hamlet is a young man. Y / N
3 Hamlet usually looks happy. Y / N
4 Ophelia loves Hamlet. Y / N
5 Hamlet's friends are worried about him. Y / N

2 **Read the information on the first page of the book. How much do you know now about the play? Match the people with the information.**

Gertrude / Hamlet's father / Claudius / Hamlet

1 _____ is Hamlet's uncle.
2 _____ was King of Denmark.
3 _____ is Hamlet's mother.
4 _____ died a short time ago.
5 _____ is still wearing black clothes.
6 _____ married Claudius a short time ago.
7 _____ can't forget his father's death.

While Reading

Read Act 1. Who said these words, and to whom?

1 'They say that ghosts never walk during the day.'
2 'Is there going to be trouble in Denmark?'
3 'Death is everywhere.'
4 'Neither a borrower nor a lender be.'
5 'I do not know what to think, my lord.'
6 'Why have you come back from the grave?'
7 'The snake that killed me now wears my crown.'
8 'There is more in this world than you can ever dream of.'

Read Act 2. Choose the best question-word for these questions, and then answer them.

How long / What / Where / Who / Why

1 . . . did Hamlet say when he visited Ophelia?
2 . . . has Hamlet known Rosencrantz and Guildenstern?
3 . . . wrote a love letter to Ophelia?
4 . . . have Rosencrantz and Guildenstern come to the castle?
5 . . . will everyone be this evening?

Read Act 3, then circle the correct words in each sentence.

1 Gertrude is *worried* / *happy* about her son.

2 Hamlet tells Ophelia that she *must* / *mustn't* marry.

3 Claudius wants Hamlet to visit *France* / *England*.

4 The ghost told Hamlet that Claudius was *a friend* / *a murderer*.

5 Claudius *enjoyed* / *didn't like* the play.

6 Hamlet stabbed *Polonius* / *the King* with his sword.

Read Act 4, then match these parts of sentences.

1 Hamlet killed Polonius

2 Claudius gave Rosencrantz and Guildenstern

3 When Hamlet left Denmark,

4 When Laertes heard about Polonius's death,

5 Claudius had a terrible surprise when

6 Claudius made a plan for

7 Gertrude told Laertes that

8 . . . a sword fight between Hamlet and Laertes.

9 . . . a letter for the King of England.

10 . . . Ophelia was dead.

11 . . . he wanted to kill Hamlet.

12 . . . and hid the body.

13 . . . Hamlet suddenly came back to Denmark.

14 . . . Rosencrantz and Guildenstern went with him.

Before you read Act 5, can you guess how the story ends? Choose Y (yes), N (no) or P (perhaps).

1 Claudius tells the truth at last. Y / N / P
2 Hamlet kills Claudius. Y / N / P
3 Hamlet is the new King of Denmark. Y / N / P
4 Laertes kills Hamlet with the poisoned sword. Y / N / P
5 Hamlet's mother dies. Y / N / P
6 Laertes is the new King of Denmark. Y / N / P

Read Act 5. Use these words from the play to complete the summary. (Use each word once.)

digging, escaped, flowers, friendly, funeral, grave, letter, plan, poison, skull

When they were coming back to the castle, Hamlet and Horatio saw a man who was _____ a _____. Hamlet found a _____ on the ground. Then the King, Gertrude and Laertes arrived for Ophelia's _____. They put her in the grave, and Gertrude put _____ on her body. Hamlet told Horatio about Claudius's _____ to the King of England. Claudius's _____ to kill him went wrong, because Hamlet _____ from the ship. Laertes and Hamlet had a sword fight. Hamlet thought it was a _____ fight – but there was _____ on Laertes' sword.

After Reading

1 **When Claudius sent Hamlet to England, he wrote a letter to the King of England (see page 28). Use these words from the play to complete the letter. (Use each word once.)**

accident, alive, careful, dangerous, father, friendly, help, immediately, kill, killed, mad, people, Polonius, Prince, Queen, tell, tried

My dear friend,

You must _____ me! I have sent _____ Hamlet to see you. Perhaps you think that Hamlet is _____ and kind – but it's not true! He is a very _____ man. He has _____ my old friend _____ – and I think he wants to _____ me too! Hamlet's _____ died a short time ago, and that made him _____. The _____ and I have _____ to help him, but we cannot. I will never be happy while Hamlet is _____. He must die!

I cannot kill Hamlet – the _____ of Denmark love him, and I must be _____. But if you kill him, I will _____ everyone that Hamlet had a terrible _____ while he was in England. Please do this for me! Kill him – _____!

Claudius

2 Perhaps this is what four characters in the play are thinking. Which characters are they, and what is happening in the play at the moment?

  1 'Oh no! Those two actors – they're showing how I killed my brother. How did they find out? I can't watch this! I must leave – now!'

  2 'Why is Hamlet so angry? He's saying terrible things to his mother. Perhaps he's going to hurt her. I must call for the guards at once!'

  3 'What's wrong with my sister? Why doesn't she remember me? Why is she singing these strange songs?'

  4 'What's happening? Why has Laertes cut my face? Isn't this a friendly fight? Well, I know what to do about that!'

3 There is one mistake in each of these sentences about the ghost. Rewrite the sentences with the correct information.

  1 The ghost of the dead King came back to speak to his brother.

  2 The guards at the castle only saw the ghost in the afternoon.

  3 The ghost told Hamlet that a snake killed him.

  4 The ghost came back when Hamlet was with Ophelia.

  5 The ghost told Hamlet not to hurt Claudius.

Do you believe in ghosts? Have you or any of your friends ever seen a ghost?

4 **What did you think about the people in the play? Choose some names, and complete some of these sentences.**

Hamlet / Ophelia / Claudius / Gertrude / Laertes / Polonius

1 I felt sorry for _____ because _____.

2 I felt angry at _____ because _____.

3 _____ was right to _____.

4 _____ was wrong to _____.

5 I think _____ did a bad thing when _____.

6 I think _____ did a good thing when _____.

5 **Find the answers to this crossword in the play.**

1 A large piece of cloth, usually over a window. (7)

2 A place in the ground for a dead body. (5)

3 The opposite of 'happy'. (3)

4 You'll see these people at a theatre or cinema. (6)

5 The bones of your head. (5)

6 You mustn't talk about this to anyone! (6)

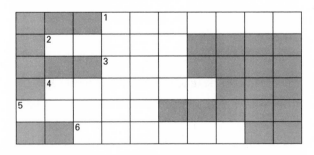

What is the hidden word in the crossword?

6 These are some words from the play. In each group, one word does not belong. Which word is it? Can you explain why?

  1 wife / son / servant / father
  2 worried / secret / happy / angry
  3 river / sword / poison / flower
  4 truth / funeral / wedding / play
  5 lend / snake / crown / bottle

7 Here is a new ending for the play. Fill in the gaps (you can use as many words as you want).

CLAUDIUS: Gertrude! Don't drink! That wine _____!
GERTRUDE: What's the matter, my love? (*She drinks from Hamlet's cup.*) Oh! This wine . . . it _____!
Gertrude falls to the floor. Everyone shouts.
HAMLET: (*Running to help her*) Mother! What's wrong?
LAERTES: There's _____ in her wine – and there's poison on _____, too. It was the King's idea!
HAMLET: (*Taking Laertes' sword*) Claudius – you murdered _____. Now I'm going to _____! (*The guards try to stop him, but he stabs Claudius.*)
HORATIO: It's true! Claudius was _____. The crown belongs to Hamlet! (*He gives the crown to Hamlet.*)
HAMLET: Laertes, we mustn't fight. Be my friend – be my adviser! You too, Horatio!

Can you think of other possible endings?

49

ABOUT THE AUTHOR

William Shakespeare (1564–1616) was born in Stratford-upon-Avon, a small town in central England. He went to school in Stratford, and he married when he was only eighteen years old. A few years later, he moved to London, while his wife and children stayed in Stratford. He worked as an actor, and soon started writing plays and poetry. At that time, theatres were new and exciting places. There were only a few theatres in England, and they were all in London.

Shakespeare wrote *Hamlet*, the most discussed work ever written for the theatre, in about 1600. A few years earlier a French writer had published the story of the tragic prince, which originally came from a 13th-century history of Denmark.

OXFORD BOOKWORMS LIBRARY

Classics • Crime & Mystery • Factfiles • Fantasy & Horror
Human Interest • Playscripts • Thriller & Adventure
True Stories • World Stories

The OXFORD BOOKWORMS LIBRARY provides enjoyable reading in English, with a wide range of classic and modern fiction, non-fiction, and plays. It includes original and adapted texts in seven carefully graded language stages, which take learners from beginner to advanced level. An overview is given on the next pages.

All Stage 1 titles are available as audio recordings, as well as over eighty other titles from Starter to Stage 6. All Starters and many titles at Stages 1 to 4 are specially recommended for younger learners. Every Bookworm is illustrated, and Starters and Factfiles have full-colour illustrations.

The OXFORD BOOKWORMS LIBRARY also offers extensive support. Each book contains an introduction to the story, notes about the author, a glossary, and activities. Additional resources include tests and worksheets, and answers for these and for the activities in the books. There is advice on running a class library, using audio recordings, and the many ways of using Oxford Bookworms in reading programmes. Resource materials are available on the website <www.oup.com/bookworms>.

The *Oxford Bookworms Collection* is a series for advanced learners. It consists of volumes of short stories by well-known authors, both classic and modern. Texts are not abridged or adapted in any way, but carefully selected to be accessible to the advanced student.

You can find details and a full list of titles in the *Oxford Bookworms Library Catalogue* and *Oxford English Language Teaching Catalogues*, and on the website <www.oup.com/bookworms>.

THE OXFORD BOOKWORMS LIBRARY
GRADING AND SAMPLE EXTRACTS

STARTER • 250 HEADWORDS
present simple – present continuous – imperative –
can/cannot, must – *going to* (future) – simple gerunds …

Her phone is ringing – but where is it?

Sally gets out of bed and looks in her bag. No phone. She looks under the bed. No phone. Then she looks behind the door. There is her phone. Sally picks up her phone and answers it. *Sally's Phone*

STAGE 1 • 400 HEADWORDS
… past simple – coordination with *and*, *but*, *or* –
subordination with *before*, *after*, *when*, *because*, *so* …

I knew him in Persia. He was a famous builder and I worked with him there. For a time I was his friend, but not for long. When he came to Paris, I came after him – I wanted to watch him. He was a very clever, very dangerous man. *The Phantom of the Opera*

STAGE 2 • 700 HEADWORDS
… present perfect – *will* (future) – *(don't) have to, must not, could* –
comparison of adjectives – simple *if* clauses – past continuous –
tag questions – *ask/tell* + infinitive …

While I was writing these words in my diary, I decided what to do. I must try to escape. I shall try to get down the wall outside. The window is high above the ground, but I have to try. I shall take some of the gold with me – if I escape, perhaps it will be helpful later. *Dracula*

... should, may – present perfect continuous – *used to* – past perfect –
causative – relative clauses – indirect statements ...

Of course, it was most important that no one should see
Colin, Mary, or Dickon entering the secret garden. So Colin
gave orders to the gardeners that they must all keep away
from that part of the garden in future. **The Secret Garden**

STAGE 4 • 1400 HEADWORDS

... past perfect continuous – passive (simple forms) –
would conditional clauses – indirect questions –
relatives with *where/when* – gerunds after prepositions/phrases ...

I was glad. Now Hyde could not show his face to the world
again. If he did, every honest man in London would be proud
to report him to the police. **Dr Jekyll and Mr Hyde**

STAGE 5 • 1800 HEADWORDS

... future continuous – future perfect –
passive (modals, continuous forms) –
would have conditional clauses – modals + perfect infinitive ...

If he had spoken Estella's name, I would have hit him. I was so
angry with him, and so depressed about my future, that I could
not eat the breakfast. Instead I went straight to the old house.
Great Expectations

STAGE 6 • 2500 HEADWORDS

... passive (infinitives, gerunds) – advanced modal meanings –
clauses of concession, condition

When I stepped up to the piano, I was confident. It was as if I
knew that the prodigy side of me really did exist. And when I
started to play, I was so caught up in how lovely I looked that
I didn't worry how I would sound. **The Joy Luck Club**

Romeo and Juliet

WILLIAM SHAKESPEARE

Retold by Alistair McCallum

What's in a name? Does it really matter if you are called Montague or Capulet? When Romeo, son of Lord and Lady Montague, falls in love with the most beautiful girl he's ever seen, he finds out that it does matter. It makes all the difference in the world, because both families hate each other bitterly.

For a time, Romeo and Juliet manage to keep their love secret. But when Romeo is sent away from Verona, and arrangements are made for Juliet to marry Paris, a friend of her father's, hope begins to die. Can any of their friends help the young lovers to be together for ever?

The Importance of Being Earnest

OSCAR WILDE

Retold by Susan Kingsley

Algernon knows that his friend Jack does not always tell the truth. For example, in town his name is Ernest, while in the country he calls himself Jack. And who is the girl who gives him presents 'from little Cecily, with all her love'?

But when the beautiful Gwendolen Fairfax says that she can only love a man whose name is Ernest, Jack decides to change his name, and become Ernest forever. Then Cecily agrees to marry Algernon, but only if his name is Ernest, too, and things become a little difficult for the two young men.

This famous play by Oscar Wilde is one of the finest comedies in the English language.